SCRIPTURE IN STYLE:

A Guide to Memorizing Scripture According to Your Learning Style

By Hannah Armbruster

Copyright Page

© 2021 Hannah Armbruster
Scripture In Style

First Printing

All rights reserved. Reproduction in whole or part without written permission from the publisher or author is strictly prohibited. Printed in the United States of America.

This book is inspired by the Holy Spirit,
Who teaches us all things.

All Scripture is taken from several versions of the Holy Bible, public domain

Hannah Armbruster
Philadelphia, Pennsylvania

Cover design by Emilie Nuñez, Bethlehem, PA

Simply This Publishing
Kindle Direct Publishing

DEDICATION PAGE

I write to all of the readers who feel hopeless when it comes to scripture memory. May you be encouraged by Jesus Christ, who has died on the cross to give you abundant life (John 10:10), especially when it comes to scripture memory!

The thief cometh not, but for to steal, and to kill, and to destroy: I am come that they might have life, and that they might have it more abundantly.

TABLE OF CONTENTS

INTRODUCTION

When you think of scripture memory, what comes to mind? Do you think of dozens of flashcards with verses written on them? Or maybe you think of having a verse pop into your head, but you just cannot remember the reference when you need it most! Or maybe, if you are like me, you think of your younger days in Sunday school when your teacher would share a verse that went with the lesson of the day and you would go home, work on memorizing it, and then come back the next week and recite it to him/her. It was a satisfying experience because you received a sticker or a prize for your efforts.

On the contrary, maybe you feel like you do not have a good memory, and that scripture memory is only for people with photographic memories, or for people who are really smart and are good at studying. If this is how you feel currently, or have felt in the past, I believe God really wants to speak to you specifically and let you know that this is a lie from the enemy, Satan, who seeks to steal, kill, and destroy (John 10:10). He wants you to believe that scripture memory is too lofty of a task and one that you are incapable of. I know it to be true because I hear it when I ask people if I can recite some verses that I have memorized to them. They comment, "Wow, that is so amazing that you can do that. I could never memorize scripture like that - my memory is not that good."

The reality is that we need to bring those lies into the light of God's Word to expose them. The Bible says that for all of those who have put their trust in Jesus Christ as Lord and Savior of their lives, they have the mind of Christ (1 Corinthians 2:16). This means that for followers of Christ who have the Holy Spirit residing in their being, they can discern the things of God because they have received the very Spirit of God within them.

Jesus says, *"I came that they may have life, and have it abundantly"* (John 10:10 ESV). He wants us to have the abundant life of favor and blessing that only He can provide in all areas of our lives, and this includes what we believe about our minds and our ability to retain the living Word of God. I believe today God wants to breathe new life into your perspective about memorizing scripture. Right now, you can pray and repent of your past mindset and then declare verbally each day, *"I have the mind of Christ that allows me to memorize scripture!"*

Now that the enemy's lies have been brought into the light and the darkness has been exposed, you may be thinking, that is great! I believe that I can memorize scripture, but I do not know where to begin and I have never had a go-to strategy that worked for me to memorize anything, even in school. Well, you are in the right place my friend; continue reading!

Being an educator, as well as a tutor and an academic coach, I work with students both young and old every day in my career. I have found that it is hard for students to learn new information when it is not presented in a way that suits their learning style. Let me give you an example: You are in a chemistry class where the teacher gives lectures each day and you have to take notes, and then read several chapters of the textbook for homework each night. You do not have any labs to reinforce the concepts you are learning - the learning is primarily done through spoken and written word. If you are a person who learns new concepts best through doing activities where you can hold the materials in your hands and manipulate them, then chances are you would not be very successful in this class. However, if you are a person who learns new concepts best through listening and/or reading the words in a textbook, then you would probably be successful in this chemistry class.

Research shows us that there are actually three types of learning modalities: visual, auditory, and kinesthetic. In the coming chapters, each learning modality will be explained in depth, but here I will briefly explain each modality. If you are a visual learner, you learn best through things that you can see, whether that be through reading graphics, images, or watching a demonstration, to name a few. If you are an auditory learner, you learn best through things that you can hear. Auditory learners learn best through having things told to them, whether that be through a lecture or a podcast, or just through ordinary conversation. Finally, kinesthetic learners learn best through being able to engage their bodies as well as their minds, whether that be through building or creating something, or doing a hands-on activity.

You may not be seeing how this relates to scripture memory, but the premise is that if you know which learning modality, or style, is specific to the way you as an individual learn, you can apply that knowledge to help you successfully memorize scripture. In order for you to determine what your learning style is in a simple way, I have included a short survey that you can take to show you whether you are primarily a visual, auditory, or kinesthetic learner. Please take some time to complete the following survey.

LEARNING STYLE SURVEY

Directions: Read each question and circle which letter best describes you. Do not overthink it!

1. If I need to build a desk, I prefer to....
    - A. See pictures of each step
    - B. Hear the instructions told to me
    - C. Be shown by someone else and then repeat after him/her

2. When I have free time, I would rather....
    - A. Draw, paint, or color
    - B. Listen to an audiobook
    - C. Play a sport

3. When I am studying for a test, I would prefer...
    - A. To write down notes from the textbook and review them
    - B. To have a study group that I can discuss content with
    - C. To take a walk while reviewing flashcards

4. When it comes to work, I would prefer...
    - A. A job where I can use my creativity and design new things
    - B. A job where I can be around people and share my ideas
    - C. A job where I can do hands-on work

5. When making a new food, I prefer....
    A. To have the recipe on paper and see
        a picture of the final product
    B. To make it with a friend where we
        can talk through each step
    C. To make it myself from scratch

6. When planting a flower, I prefer....
    A. To look at a list of supplies and set
        everything out before beginning
    B. To listen to music in the
        background or hum
    C. To get my hands dirty and dig in
        the soil

7. When doing classwork, I prefer to...
    A. Read the textbook and see images
        of what I am learning
    B. Hear a lecture or presentation
    C. Interact with materials so that I can
        touch and feel them

8. When I need to remember someone's name, I
    prefer to...
    A. Write it down
    B. Repeat it aloud to myself three
        times
    C. Pair the name with an action

9. When I need directions, I prefer to...
    A. Write them down
    B. Hear them being spoken aloud
    C. Talk to myself and say, *"Turn right here."*

10. When it is a friend's birthday, I prefer to...
    A. Make him/her a photo album with pictures
    B. Call him/her on the phone and sing *"Happy Birthday"* to hear his/her reaction
    C. Go over to his/her house and surprise him/her

11. When I have an argument with someone, I prefer to...
    A. Write him/her a note of apology
    B. Verbally express why I was wrong
    C. Give him/her a gift as a way to say, *"I'm sorry"*

<u>Results:</u> If you have circled mostly A's, you are probably a visual learner. If you have circled mostly B's, you are probably an auditory learner. If you have circled mostly C's, then chances are you are probably a kinesthetic learner. If you circled the same number of any two letters, this indicates that you learn best through using both of those learning styles.

WHY MEMORIZE ANYWAY?

Now that you have found out what your learning style is, you may be asking yourself the logical question, *"Why memorize scripture?"* and furthermore, you might ask yourself, *"Why is it necessary to memorize scripture when I have my Bible app at my fingertips on my phone?"* I find the answer to this question is a simple one - God never asks us to hide His Word in our phones, but instead to hide His word in our hearts. Psalm 119:11 says, *"I have stored up your word in my heart, that I might not sin against you"* (ESV). The author of Psalm 119 is unknown, but a lot of commentators agree that this is a Psalm of David. If we look at David, one of the most prolific writers of the Psalms, he is deemed a *"man after God's own heart."* Why is he called this? His actions consistently show that even when he makes mistakes, he repents, and he earnestly desires to obey the commands of God. How did David know what the commands of God were? He read them in the Torah, and he became well acquainted with them. In Psalm 119:10 David says, *"With my whole heart I seek you; let me not wander from your commandments!"* (ESV) and in Psalm 119:20 he says, *"My soul is consumed with longing for your rules at all times"* (ESV).

I recently read the account of David in 1 Samuel 26 when he was on the run from King Saul, a man who earnestly sought to kill David because he knew that God had rejected his kingship and had designated David to be the next king of Israel. As I read this chapter, one particular thing that David says to Saul caught my attention. He says, *"...They [David's enemies] have driven me out this day that I should have no share in the heritage of the Lord, saying, 'Go, serve other gods.'"* (1 Samuel 26:19, ESV). While

David was on the run, he did not go to the house of the Lord out of fear that someone would recognize him and report his location to King Saul. Commentator David Guzik writes, "What hurts David the most is that he can't go to the house of God, and openly be with the people of God, and live his life after the LORD as he longs to."[1] David expresses his sorrow at not being able to openly go into the house of God. Why is this so significant? Think about why going to church each week is significant for you. If I could guess, I would say it is because you get to 1) Hear the Word of God being preached and 2) You encounter your brothers and sisters in Christ, allowing for mutual encouragement, community, and partnership in sharing the Gospel. If you do not have access to a church, you do not have access to the preaching of the Word or church community. Oftentimes, when the enemy can get you alone and away from your

Christian brothers and sisters, he uses the opportunity to tell you lies such as, *"God does not really care about you. Look, He let you get into this hopeless situation,"* or *"You are not lovable because of what you have done."* When this happens, if you have a community of people who personally know Jesus around you, they will help you point out these lies, and remind you of the truths found in the Bible. These two elements of hearing the Word preached and having community are both essential elements that are needed for growing and continuing on in your faith. When David was on the run, he did not have access to either of these elements. It was imperative that he had the scriptures hidden in his heart so he could easily recall them during trying times.

One well-known man who was able to hold onto God's Word in the midst of trying times is George Müller. He lived in the early 1800's, and God placed in him a desire to care for, educate, and share the gospel with the many orphans in Bristol, England. This was a man who was certainly not well off, but through prayer, held God to the promises found in His Word. He solely depended on God to provide for all of the needs that the orphans under his care had, without ever mentioning to any fellow human that he was in need. Müller wrote in his journal, "He [God] is their [the orphans] Father, and therefore has pledged Himself, as it were, to provide for them; and I have only to remind Him of the need of these poor children in order to have it supplied."[2] Müller noted this after he was doing his Bible reading and came across Psalm 68:5 where God is named the *"Father of the fatherless"*. George always prioritized his time with God through reading the scriptures and praying on his knees in the morning. This reminded him where his identity was found, and it allowed him to keep his eyes fixed on the faithful provision of God at a time when others around him were forsaking their time with God both independently and corporately in order to work longer hours to provide for their families. He held onto God's Word fervently, therefore cultivating an intimate relationship with Him and displaying ultimate trust in Him at a time when many others around him did not orient their lives around the principles found in God's Word.

When the Psalmist says, *"I have stored up your word in my heart"* (Psalm 119:11 ESV), the words *stored up* in Hebrew are *tsaphan*, which means "to hide, treasure"; "by implication, to hoard or reserve;" "to store up."[3] The first part of this definition (to hide, treasure) has to do with the idea that scripture should be hidden because it is valuable. The Christian should value the Word of God similarly to how a person values and treasures his money. For example, it does not make much sense for a person to keep his savings of $5,000 in plain sight in the kitchen. Why? It is much too valuable to keep it where it can be seen and potentially stolen. Most people would say that it makes more sense to hide or store up money in a safe or in a specially marked place where it will be secure. Likewise, the Christian should value the Word of God like money in the sense that it is a valuable tool, and therefore, ought to be kept in a safe place, namely the heart, where no one can steal it.

The second part of the definition *tsaphan* (to hoard or reserve) has to do with the idea that memorizing scripture is something that is used in times of emergency. People create reserves and hoard materials so that they will have plenty of a particular item. Relating it once again to money, a person could store up $300 in his emergency fund. If a negative circumstance came along, such as getting a flat tire and needing a repair, he could fix that problem with the $300. However, if he ended up in the hospital and his bill came out to be $10,000, he would not have any money available in his fund to pay for the expenses. Is having $300 bad? No, for it will come in handy for small emergencies. Similarly, if you see each verse memorized as being worth $300 that you have in your pocket that might be beneficial for waging the day to day battles the enemy throws up against you. However, when you cherish the Word and memorize dozens of verses, it is like building up a large emergency fund. In a time of trial and tribulation the benefit of knowing much scripture will be your saving grace through the season. Just as having a large emergency fund does not mean you will never have a spur of the moment emergency, having a lot of verses memorized does not mean you will never have any trials in life. It just means that you can have peace in each season, knowing that you have a storehouse of verses piled up in the *"emergency fund"* of your heart.

The final part of the definition *tsaphan* that I will touch on is to "store up". The Dictionary of Biblical Imagery comments on this idea by saying, "Storing up is essentially an image of gradual accumulation."[4] In short, people store up objects when they will need to access them later. I think about Joseph and how he prepared Egypt for the seven years of famine in the land by telling the servants under him to build storehouses to hold grain enough to last the country through the famine. He put grain in the storehouses in advance so that the citizens would have access to it when the time came. It took a lot of time and dedication to store up food enough to feed the people of an entire country for seven years. In the same way, storing up the Word of God in your heart is a process that often takes weeks, months, years, and much dedication. While it may seem somewhat foreign to us, storing up the Word was not uncommon in the Jewish culture. "At the ages of six through twelve, the Jewish boys and girls would begin their education in synagogue school, learning how to read and write. The textbook was the Torah (the first five books of the Bible) and the goal was to memorize the sacred text."[5] The good news for you is that nobody is requiring you to memorize the whole Bible in six years! Memorization can be done little by little, until you realize that you have a storehouse of verses piled up in your heart.

One benefit of having a storehouse of verses hidden in your heart is so that you might not sin against God (Psalm 119:11). Jesus modeled this for us perfectly when He was tempted in the wilderness for 40 days. The sole weapon that He used to combat the lies of Satan was the written Word of God. Each time, Jesus replied to Satan by saying, *"It is written..."* and then He quoted the scriptures. Jesus proved that the Word of God has the power to combat the lies of the enemy. We know this because when He was in the wilderness, He stripped himself of all other necessities (i.e. food, water, shelter) and let the Word of God be His only life sustainer. It certainly made the enemy flee quickly! Hebrews 4:12 speaks of the power of the Word of God: *"For the word of God is living and active, sharper than any two-edged sword, piercing to the division of soul and of spirit, of joints and of marrow, and discerning the thoughts and intentions of the heart"* (ESV). It is living and active solely because God is alive! God can speak only truth, and the very words He utters are the only words with authority sharp enough to pierce through the lies and darkness that the enemy uses to get you to sin.

Apostle John speaks along the same lines by saying, *"I write to you, young men, because you are strong, and the word of God abides in you, and you have overcome the evil one"* (1 John 2:14 ESV). These men are strong because the Word of God abides in them. The word abides has the idea of continually residing with something. When pieces of God's Word reside with you all the time, you are able to quickly pull them out in defense when the enemy tempts you, just as Jesus did in the wilderness. To neglect scripture memory is to reject one of the most powerful pieces of spiritual armor - the sword of the Spirit (Ephesians 6:17). Do you see it? The word *sword* has *"word"* in it! God has given us access to His Word, which is a sharp and powerful sword during this time in our lives. We cannot afford to go another day without it.

Being denied the freedom to access the written Word of God may seem far-fetched in these present days where we have the freedom to corporately meet in churches (well, in these days of COVID-19, mostly online!) and most of us probably have at least three copies of the Bible laying around our houses. But church, wake up! We need to be alert to the times we are living in. A time may be coming in the United States when we will not have the freedom to access the written Word of God. After all, in many countries in the world, namely North Korea, China, Afghanistan, Somalia, Libya, and Pakistan, it is illegal to admit you are a follower of Jesus and/or openly read your Bible today.

According to Open Doors, a ministry which exists to strengthen persecuted Christians all over the world, two of the many sources of persecution are communist oppression and oppression by radical Islamists.[6] Once a Communist regime or a radical Islamic group is given supreme power in a country, the result is often Christians losing the right to openly practice their faith in the one true God of the Bible. For example, one primary means of practicing the Christian faith is through reading the Bible. For the courageous Christians who do take the risk of reading their Bibles or talking about the Gospel in public, the consequences are steep and can be in the form of disownment from family members, time in prison, work in labor camps, starvation, assault, denial from the markets, the community, or worst of all, death. (To find out more, go on Open Doors' website and read some of the true stories of Christians who have been persecuted).

In America, we are blessed not to face this type of persecution, and most of us have no idea how it feels to be put in prison or a labor camp for simply practicing our faith by going to church, reading our Bibles in public, or evangelizing in public. In one sense this is because thus far in America, there has never been one primary, overarching political party or religion in power that has oppressed people of all other religions or ways of thinking. Even so, we should not rule this scenario out as something that could never happen in the future. We have seen candidates in the mix of politicians running for president who believe in socialist ideals, which are very closely tied to Communist ideals. Communist leaders are known for severely rejecting and punishing people who hold ideologies that are in opposition to those of their party. We have seen this scenario played out in countries in the past.

For example, during the Cold War, Bibles were banned and burned. This was a result of Christianity being seen as a threat to the opposing belief system that was vying for dominance. Brother Andrew, whose story is told in the book, *God's Smuggler*, was a missionary who courageously smuggled Bibles behind the Iron Curtain during the Cold War. He felt called into several of these Communist countries in which religious belief was persecuted, so that people would have access to the written Word of God. Brother Andrew quotes Revelation 3:2, which is *"Wake up! Strengthen what remains and is about to die,"* as the pinnacle passage for his calling to serve the Persecuted Church.[7] Who is to say that the culture of the United States will not come to a place in its rapidly declining morality when *"what remains"*, namely the Word of God and the principles of God, are *"about to die"*, or are cast aside and unheeded?

When we look at the context of this verse in Revelation, it is a command to the church at Sardis. This is what has been said about the church at Sardis:

"The connection between Sardis and money -

easy money - was well known in the ancient

world...It had a well-deserved reputation for apathy and immortality...The combination of easy money and a loose moral environment made the people of Sardis notoriously soft and pleasure loving...Its people were notoriously loose-living, notoriously pleasure-and luxury loving."[8]

When I read this description of Sardis, I think of my own beloved country, the United States of America. 1 Timothy 6:10 says, *"For the love of money is a root of all kinds of evils. It is through this craving that some have wandered away from the faith and pierced themselves with many pangs"* (ESV). So that there is no confusion - the verse does NOT say money is the root of all kinds of evil; it says the LOVE of money. The culture in America says that we ought to get an education in order to get the best job we can, in order to make the most amount of money we can. The

"American Dream" that so many aspire towards is one that desires softness and luxury. This is a dangerous place to be in as it allows us to be lulled to sleep, when the scriptures tell us to, *"Wake up, O Sleeper"* and STAY awake (Eph 5:14, Romans 13:11-14)!

Jesus speaks to this desire for softness and luxury when He tells the parable of the rich fool in Luke 12:13-21. This was a man whose crops produced a plentiful harvest. The man soon "thought to himself, *'What shall I do, for I have no place to store my crops?'" He goes on to say, "'I will do this: I will tear down my barns and build larger ones, and there I will store all my grain and goods'. And I will say to my soul, 'Soul, you have ample goods laid up for many years; relax, eat, drink, be merry.' But God said to him, 'Fool! This night your soul is required of you...'"* (ESV). At first glance, what this man did does not seem harmless. He is just building bigger barns so that he has enough room for his grain. BUT...the problem here is that his focus was not on building God's Kingdom, but on building his own earthly kingdom, which was quickly taken from him when it was his time to die. It is important to make a distinction here - storing up things is not sinful. However, if what you store up replaces God in your life, that thing becomes an idol in your life. Instead, we must store up things that magnify God in our lives, such as scripture. Jesus warns the church in Sardis by saying, *"'I have not found your works complete in the sight of my God...if you will not wake up, I will come like a thief, and you will not know at what hour I will come against you'"* (Revelation 3:2-3 ESV). This is very similar to how death came like a thief upon the rich fool in the parable. If Americans continue having this mindset where they esteem money and riches, it will not be long before they are lulled asleep, and their life required of them, just like the decline came upon the church at Sardis, and death came like a thief upon the rich fool in the parable.

What would you do if you were David and you were on the run, having no way to read your Bible or hear the Word being preached? We have already experienced a season during COVID-19 when we were not allowed to gather at our local churches for the safety of the congregation. It was heartbreaking for many of us not having the opportunity to see our church family who we love dearly, in person. If there was no technology to watch a live streamed service, or to listen to a podcast, or watch a sermon on TV, we would have to rely on our own reading of the scriptures. But what would happen if we had no access to our churches, no access to our physical Bibles, no access to our Bibles on our devices, and Christian ideals were disregarded by the government? The Word would surely need to be *stored up* in our hearts.

DEVELOPING A MEMORIZING SESSION

Now that you have an understanding of why scripture memory is of utmost importance, I want to make some recommendations about how a session of scripture memory could look. It is important to emphasize here that for each person a session will look different, and naturally one season in life may yield more time for scripture memory sessions than others. That's *o-kay*! The important part is that you are taking any time that you can afford to store up God's Word in your heart so that you have a defense against the enemy. So, without further adieu, here we go!

- **Begin Your Session in Prayer.** We previously talked about how we as Christians have the mind of Christ (1 Cor. 2:16). We have the Holy Spirit living inside of us, who illuminates and helps us understand the scriptures as we read them. The Holy Spirit also brings the Word of God to our minds when we need to remember it. In John 14:26 Jesus says, *"But the Helper, the Holy Spirit, whom the Father will send in my name, he will teach you all things and bring to your remembrance all that I have said to you"* (ESV). Because of this truth, I always like to start off my session with prayer, asking the Holy Spirit to bring to mind the verses I have already learned, and to help me remember what I will learn that day.

- **Choosing a Version.** Most Christians have a specific version of the Bible that they prefer to read. It is important to remember that originally, the Old Testament was written in Hebrew and Aramaic, and the

New Testament was originally written in Greek. Some translators of the Bible, "attempt to produce as literal a translation as possible," while "others try to carry the meaning from the original to English." "However, because the original languages are so different than English, a direct translation sometimes sounds a bit 'wooden' and not as smooth as native English might sound."[9] You just have to consider if you want a more literal translation or a more *"flowing"* translation. Some examples of a more literal translation are the English Standard Version (ESV), the New American Standard Bible (NASB), and the King James Version (KJV). An example of a more flowing version would be the New International Version (NIV). If you look at the same verse in each of the versions, you will find that the wording is very similar throughout all of them.

- **Start Small.** Memorize one or two verses at a time. Too many at once can be overwhelming. Start with verses that have been impactful to you recently and can be applied to your current situation. You can also pick some verses that pertain to a specific topic that you have been pondering, such as redemption, the love of God, or the fruit of the Spirit. Another way to memorize is through chunking two or three verses[10] so that memorizing a section, or a chapter of scripture is more manageable.

- **Fall Asleep to Scripture Memory**. As a child, you probably were told that if you are not able to fall asleep you can count sheep and then you will eventually doze off. Well, there is a better solution to nights where you do not drift off into sleep immediately! Recite the verses that you have been memorizing recently in your head. It is a great way to see if you have retained what you practiced earlier in the day, and I have found that every time I have done this, I have just dozed off into sleep midway through. In addition, if you do not fancy the idea of reciting the verses in your head, you could use a Bible app on your phone and listen to someone else reading the passage you have been memorizing as you fall asleep. The Word of God brings peace and comfort in a way that counting sheep cannot.

In conclusion, this is just a brief overview of how a memorizing session could look. Remember, memorization is a very personalized experience. Pick and choose what method works best for you! For the remainder of the book, I will take a deep dive *In Style* to provide practical strategies for each type of learner.

IN STYLE: VISUAL LEARNERS

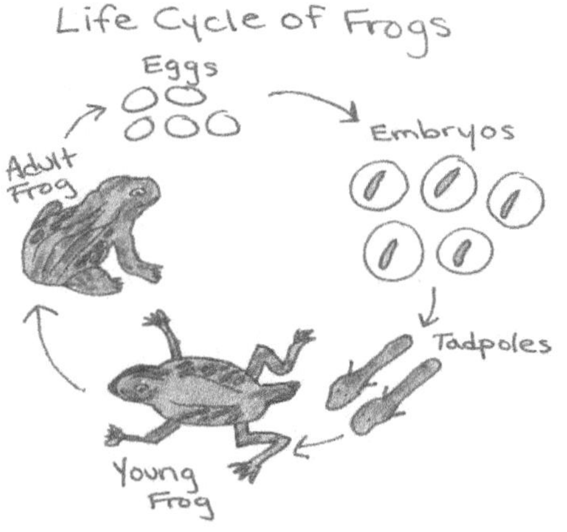

Visual learners primarily learn new content through things that they can see with their eyes. They find images, photographs, charts, drawings, and diagrams particularly helpful when learning a new process or task. For example, if a visual learner is introduced to the life cycle of a frog, chances are he will learn the cycle most effectively through looking at a diagram similar to this one, where he can see each stage shown through visualization. Another example would involve trying to figure out if too many hours during the day are spent on work. A visual learner will benefit from seeing a pie graph that shows the breakdown of how his time is spent in a day. He is then able to visually see the size of each segment of the day, and the colors differentiating each daily activity will help aid his brain in distinguishing between activities.

If you are a visual learner, in school you probably learned best when you had assignments that required you to learn information that was shown through visualizations. For example, maybe you learned best through watching videos or simulations, seeing 3D objects/models, or performing experiments. Perhaps as a child you greatly enjoyed spending time by yourself reading books because you were able to learn easily as you saw the words on the page and were able to easily make sense of them. Or maybe you greatly enjoyed learning through taking notes while watching videos on how to do a task or activity since you could clearly recall the images in your mind at a later time as you reread your notes.

Visual learners are usually very "color" smart. In other words, visual learners can be very skilled with design because they often have an understanding of which colors and patterns go together, and they have great spatial awareness. Because of these skills, visual learners may be good at jobs involving fashion, sewing, interior/exterior painting, architecture, graphic design, or cooking. Having this knowledge, the rest of this chapter will be dedicated to providing examples of practical strategies for memorizing scripture that can be used by visual learners. Note: I created the following strategies as if I was working on memorizing the book of James.

👁 **Style 1:** ***Picture Memory Cards:*** These picture memory cards are meant to function like flashcards, but instead of having all words on them, they have pictures. The images on the front of the card should trigger the remembrance of one to two verses in your mind. On the back of the flashcards the verses are typed out so that once you recite the verses in your mind or aloud by looking at the pictures, you can flip the card over and check your accuracy. The goal is to be able to flip through all of the picture cards and be able to recite the whole chapter of scripture either in your mind or aloud without having to flip the cards over to look at the verses on the back. If you repetitively flip through the cards, the images on the cards will stick in your mind, so that when you go to recite Chapter 1 of James without the cards, as each image pops into your mind, you will be able to remember each verse. I purposely made the pictures using simple graphics, such as stick figure people, in order to show that you do not need to be an amazing artist to create picture cards! If memorizing the whole chapter sounds intimidating, you can easily pick out one or two picture memory cards and start by memorizing those verses.

Note: The following picture cards are printed in black and white. If you would like free access to the color version of the cards so that you can print them out and use them,
visit: https://sites.google.com/view/scriptureinstylere sources/home.

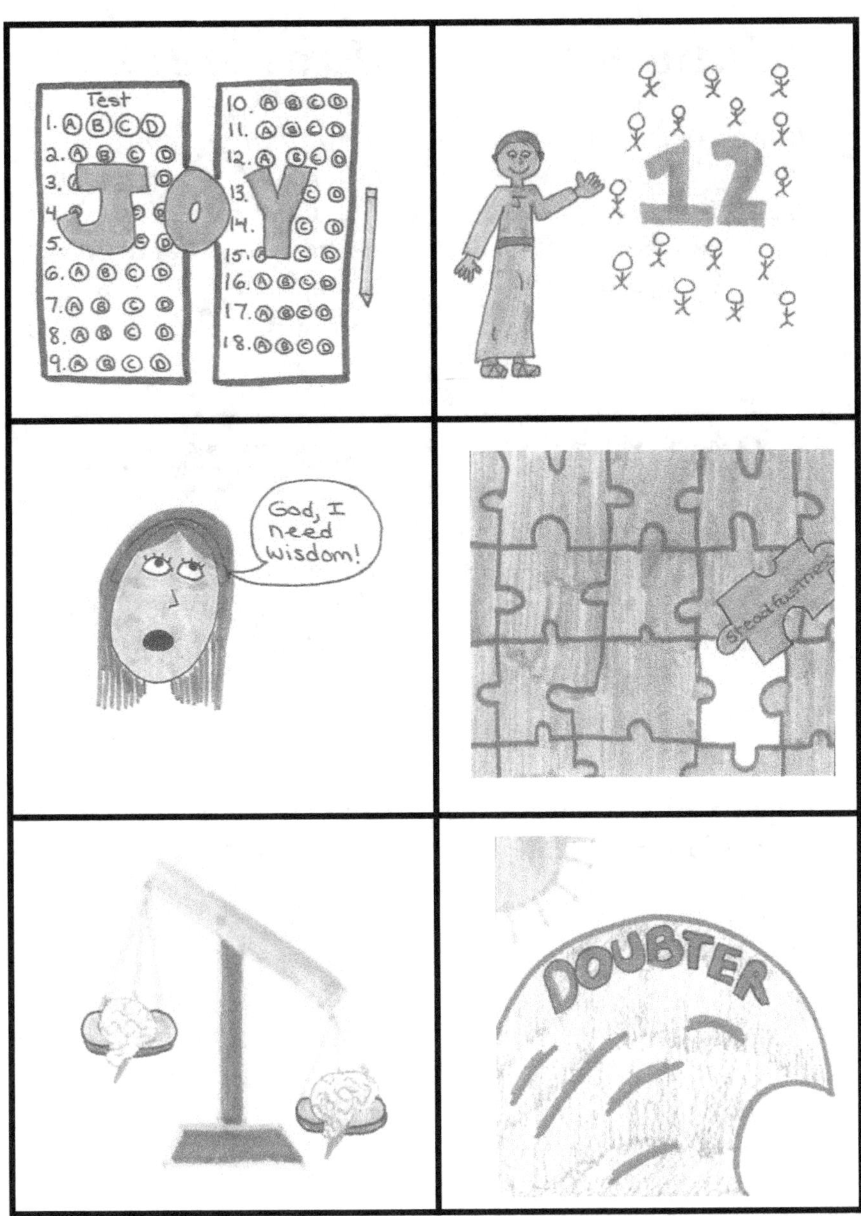

Test
God, I
need
wisdom!
DOUBTER

James 1:1

"James, a servant of God and of the Lord Jesus Christ, to the twelve tribes in the Dispersion: Greetings."

James 1:2-3

"Count it all joy, my brothers, when you meet trials of various kinds, for you know that the testing of your faith produces steadfastness."

James 1:4

"And let steadfastness have its full effect, that you may be perfect and complete, lacking in nothing."

James 1:5

"If any of you lacks wisdom, let him ask God, who gives generously to all without reproach, and it will be given to him."

James 1:6

"But let him ask in faith, with no doubting, for the one who doubts is like a wave of the sea that is driven and tossed by the wind."

James 1:7-8

"For that person must not suppose he will receive anything from the Lord; he is a double-minded man, unstable in all his ways."

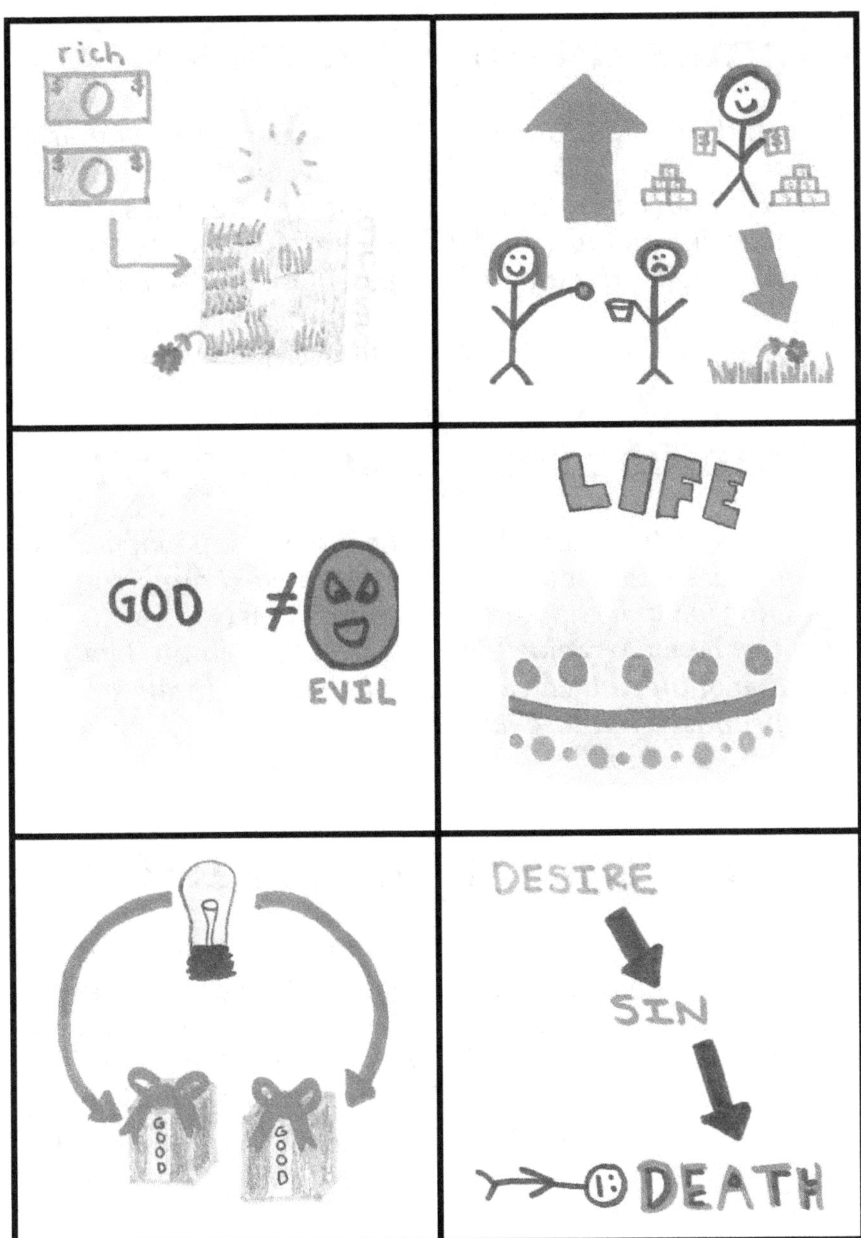
rich
GOD ≠ EVIL
LIFE
GOOD
GOOD
DESIRE
SIN
DEATH

James 1:9-10

"Let the lowly brother boast in his exaltation, and the rich in his humiliation, because like a flower of the grass he will pass away."

James 1:11

"For the sun rises with its scorching heat and withers the grass; its flower falls, and its beauty perishes. So also will the rich man fade away in the midst of his pursuits."

James 1:12

"Blessed is the man who remains steadfast under trial, for when he has stood the test he will receive the crown of life, which God has promised to those who love him."

James 1:13

"Let no one say when he is tempted, 'I am being tempted by God,' for God cannot be tempted with evil, and he himself tempts no one."

James 1:14-15

"But each person is tempted when he is lured and enticed by his own desire. Then desire when it has conceived gives birth to sin when it is fully grown brings forth death."

James 1:16-17

"Do not be deceived, my beloved brothers. Every good gift and every perfect gift is from above, coming down from the Father of lights, with whom there is no variation or shadow due to change."

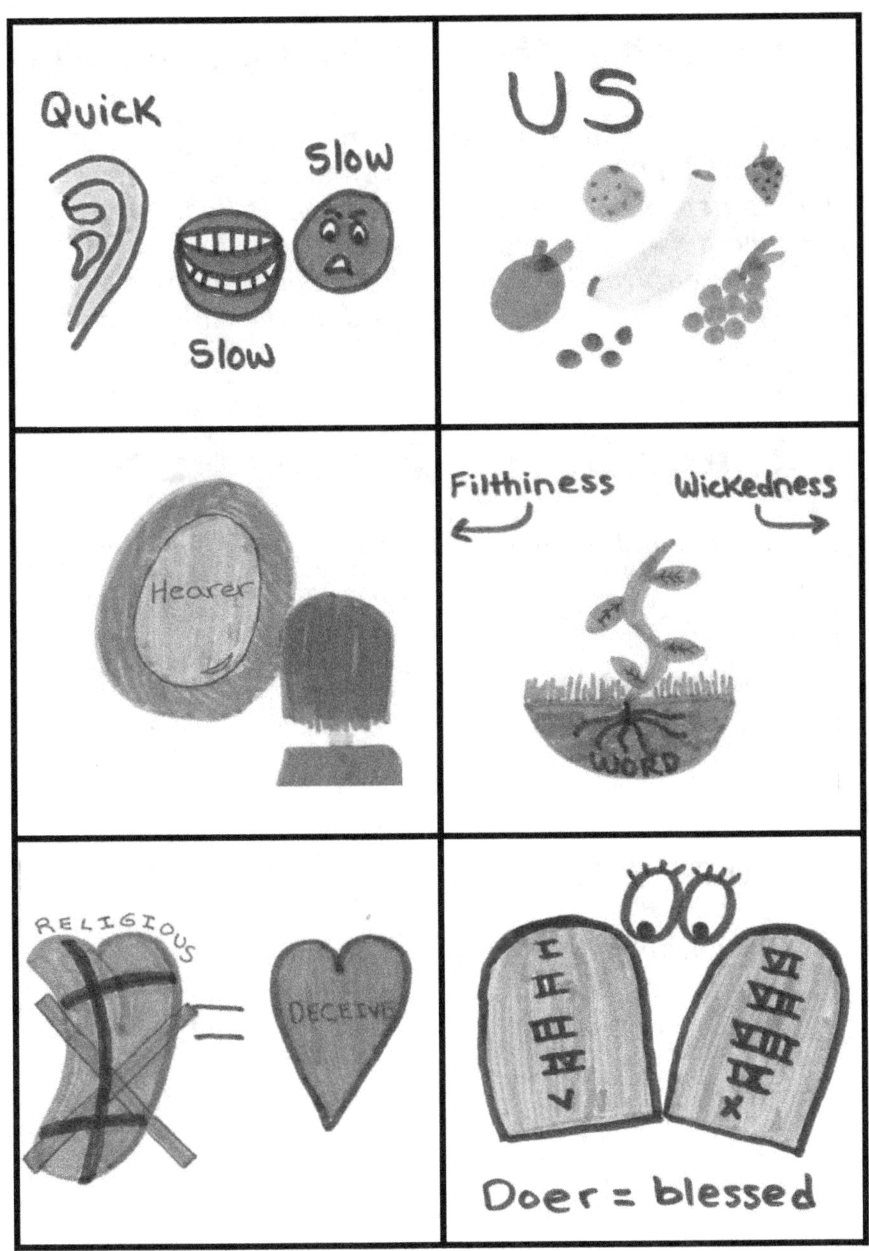

Quick
Slow
Slow
US
Hearer
Filthiness
Wickedness
WORD
RELIGIOUS
DECEIVE
Doer = blessed

James 1:18

"Of his own will he brought us forth by the word of truth, that we should be a kind of firstfruits of his creatures."

James 1:19-20

"Know this, my beloved brothers: let every person be quick to hear, slow to speak, slow to anger, for the anger of man does not produce the righteousness of God."

James 1:21

"Therefore put away all filthiness and rampant wickedness and receive with meekness the implanted word, which is able to save your souls."

James 1:22-24

"But be doers of the word, and not hearers only, deceiving yourselves. For if anyone is a hearer of the word and not a doer, he is like a man who looks intently at his natural face in a mirror. For he looks at himself and goes away and at once forgets what he was like."

James 1:25

"But the one who looks into the perfect law, the law of liberty, and perseveres, being no hearer who forgets but a doer who acts, he will be blessed in his doing."

James 1:26

"If anyone thinks he is religious and does not bridle his tongue but deceives his heart, this person's religion is worthless."

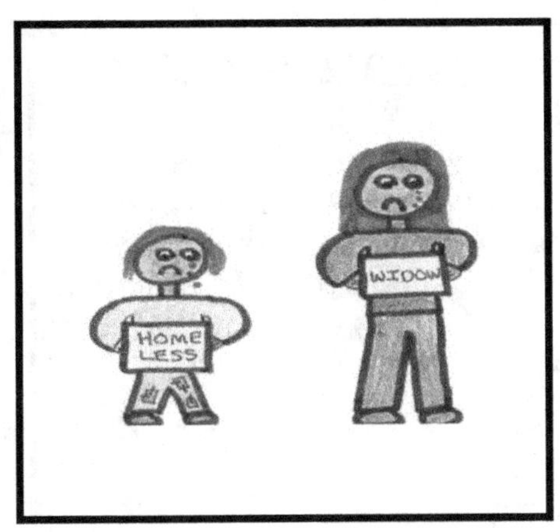

HOME
LESS
WIDOW

James 1:27

"Religion that is pure and undefiled before God the Father is this: to visit orphans and widows in their affliction, and to keep oneself unstained from the world."

TRY IT YOURSELF!
Draw, cut out, or print out images that represent four
verses of your choosing!

TRY IT YOURSELF!

Now, write down the references to each of your four
verses.

◉ **Style 2:** *Key Word Klues:* The way this strategy works is that chapter two of James is first written out in paragraph form. Then the key words in each verse are bolded and color coded so that your brain can easily remember and identify them. At first, read through the chapter a few times while looking at the pictures (klues) that go along with the key words so that you begin to associate the pictures with the words. Once you are able to identify the words that the pictures represent, then you can begin to memorize one verse at a time using the picture klues as memory aids. You will be able to go through each verse by covering up the words and just looking at the pictures to jog your memory. Eventually, if you choose, you will be able to recite the whole chapter without looking at the pictures because your brain will be able to visualize the pictures and remember which words matched the pictures. Remember, if the whole chapter is too much; start small with one or two verses!

Note: The following key word klues are printed in black and white. If you would like free access to the color version so that you can print it out and use it, visit: https://sites.google.com/view/scriptureinstyleresources/home.

The Sin of Partiality

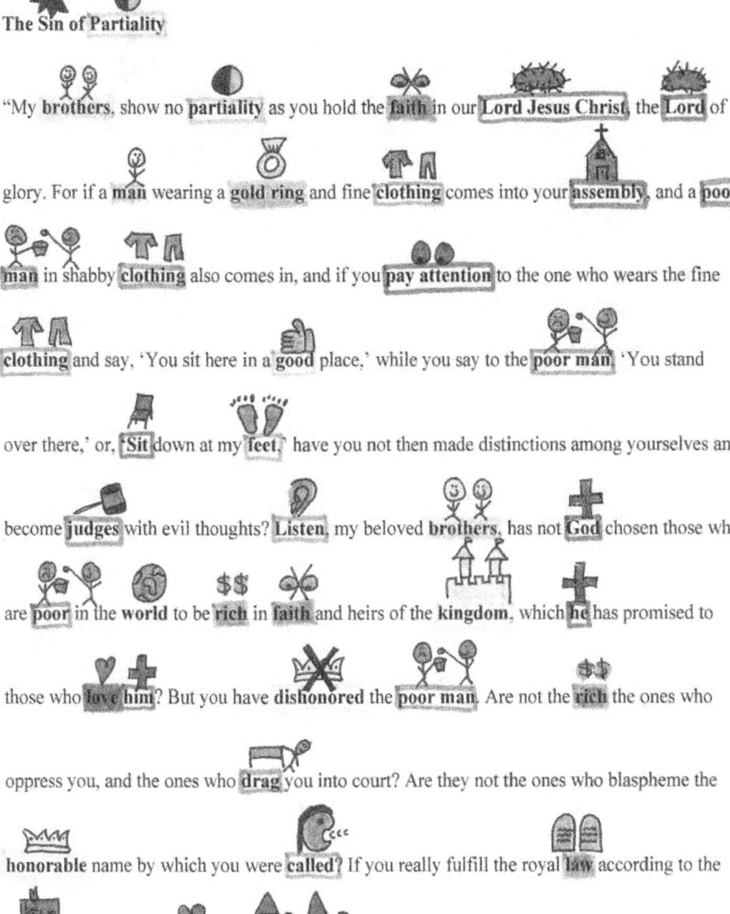

"My **brothers**, show no **partiality** as you hold the **faith** in our **Lord Jesus Christ**, the **Lord** of glory. For if a **man** wearing a **gold ring** and fine **clothing** comes into your **assembly**, and a **poor man** in shabby **clothing** also comes in, and if you **pay attention** to the one who wears the fine **clothing** and say, 'You sit here in a **good** place,' while you say to the **poor man**, 'You stand over there,' or, '**Sit** down at my **feet**,' have you not then made distinctions among yourselves and become **judges** with evil thoughts? **Listen**, my beloved **brothers**, has not **God** chosen those who are **poor** in the **world** to be **rich** in **faith** and heirs of the **kingdom**, which **he** has promised to those who **love him**? But you have **dishonored** the **poor man**. Are not the **rich** the ones who oppress you, and the ones who **drag** you into court? Are they not the ones who blaspheme the **honorable** name by which you were **called**? If you really fulfill the royal **law** according to the **Scripture**, 'You shall **love** your **neighbor** as yourself,' you are doing well. But if you show **partiality**, you are committing **sin** and are convicted by the **law** as transgressors. For whoever

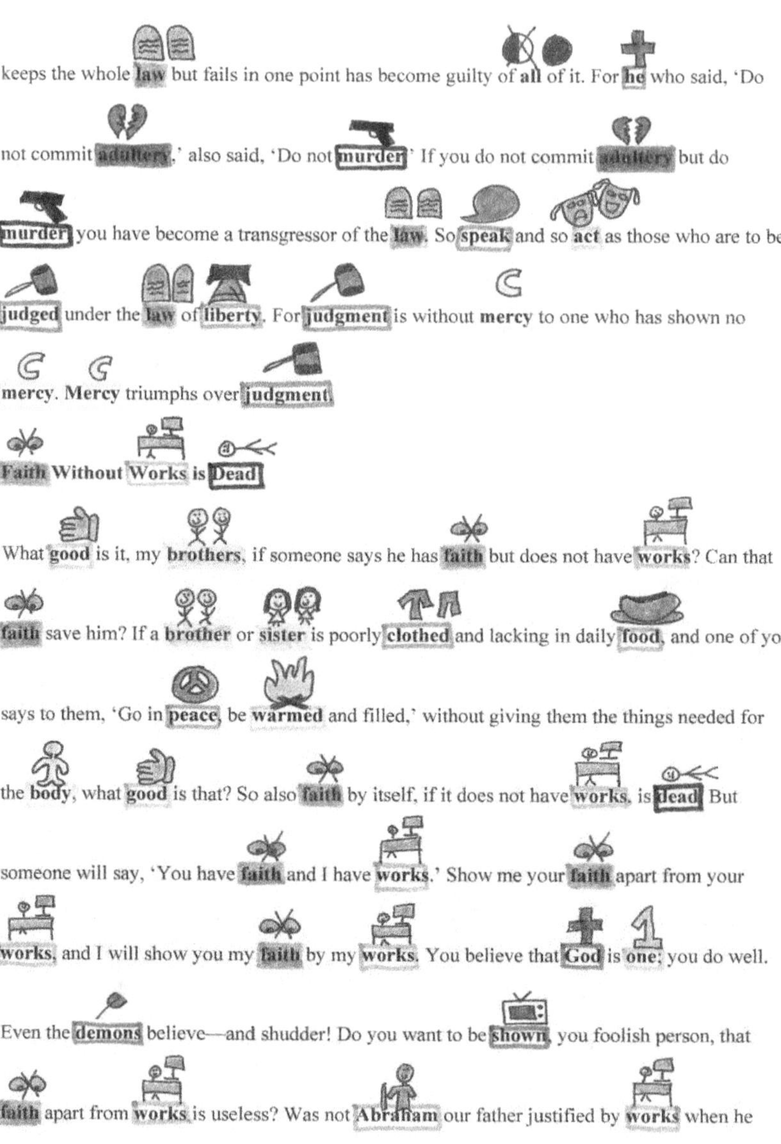

keeps the whole law but fails in one point has become guilty of all of it. For he who said, 'Do not commit adultery,' also said, 'Do not murder.' If you do not commit adultery but do murder you have become a transgressor of the law. So speak and so act as those who are to be judged under the law of liberty. For judgment is without mercy to one who has shown no mercy. Mercy triumphs over judgment.

Faith Without Works is Dead

What good is it, my brothers, if someone says he has faith but does not have works? Can that faith save him? If a brother or sister is poorly clothed and lacking in daily food, and one of you says to them, 'Go in peace, be warmed and filled,' without giving them the things needed for the body, what good is that? So also faith by itself, if it does not have works, is dead. But someone will say, 'You have faith and I have works.' Show me your faith apart from your works, and I will show you my faith by my works. You believe that God is one; you do well. Even the demons believe—and shudder! Do you want to be shown, you foolish person, that faith apart from works is useless? Was not Abraham our father justified by works when he

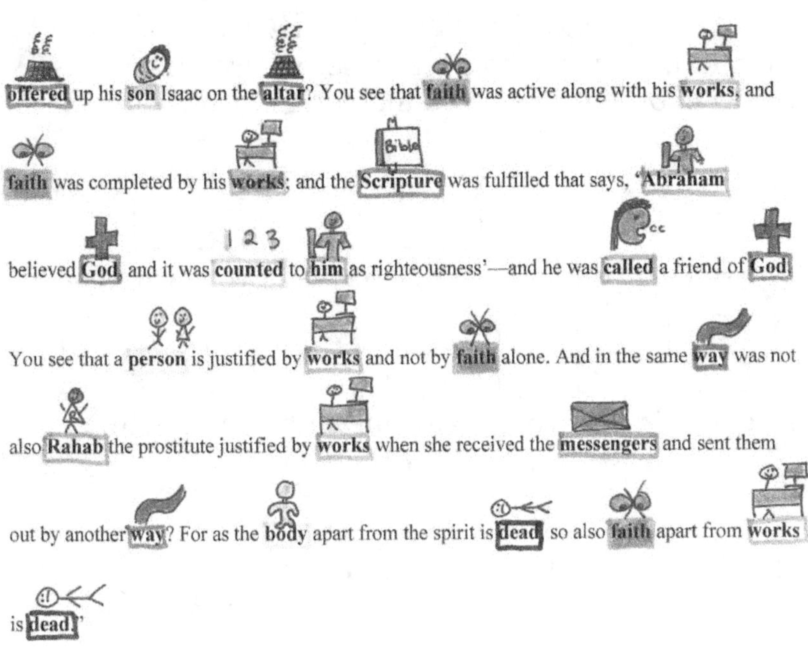

offered up his son Isaac on the altar? You see that faith was active along with his works, and faith was completed by his works; and the Scripture was fulfilled that says, 'Abraham believed God, and it was counted to him as righteousness'—and he was called a friend of God. You see that a person is justified by works and not by faith alone. And in the same way was not also Rahab the prostitute justified by works when she received the messengers and sent them out by another way? For as the body apart from the spirit is dead, so also faith apart from works is dead.'

TRY IT YOURSELF!

Create colorful symbols for these verses in the boxes
below in order to help you memorize them.

John 3:16 (ESV) "For God so loved the world, that

he gave his only Son, that whoever believes in him

should not perish but have eternal life."

Psalm 119:105 (ESV) "Your word is a lamp to my

feet and a light to my path."

1 Peter 5:7 (ESV) "Casting all your anxieties on him,

because he cares for you."

👁 **Style 3:** *Pictorial Outline:* The way this strategy works is that chapter three of James is written in typical outline form with Roman numerals, letters, and numbers. Like a typical outline, the outline contains key phrases from the chapter, and they are meant to be memory aids used to remember each verse in the chapter. The pictures serve as additional memory aids. If outlines are your style, you are able to remember the order of the content in a passage by looking at a few key phrases.

Note: The following outline is printed in black and white. If you would like free access to the color version of the outline so that you can print it out and use it, visit: https://sites.google.com/view/scriptureinstyleresources/home.

James 3

I.   We all stumble in many ways (v. 2) 

    A. Not many of us should become teachers (v. 1) 

        1. Judged with greater strictness (v. 1) 

II.   The Perfect Man

    A. Does not stumble in what he says (v. 2) 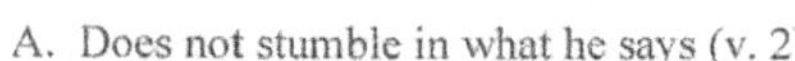

    B. Is able to bridle his whole body (v. 2) 

III.   The Small Tongue 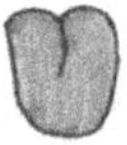

    A. Examples

        a. Bits in horses' mouths (v. 3) 

            i. We guide their whole bodies (v. 3) 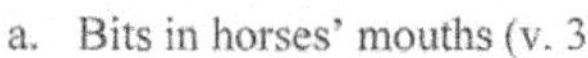

        b. Ships 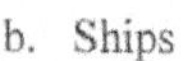 

            i. Large and driven by strong winds (v. 4) 

            ii. Guided by a small rudder (v. 4) 

    B. Likewise...The tongue is a small member (v. 5) 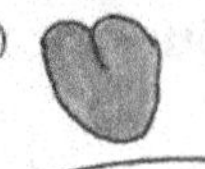

        a. It boasts of great things (v. 5) 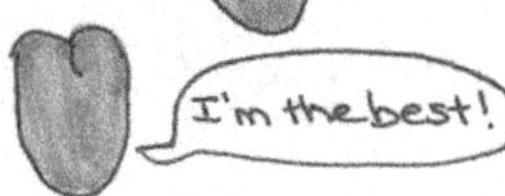

IV.   Characteristics of the Tongue

    A. A fire (v. 5) 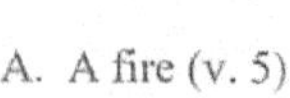 

        a. A great forest is set ablaze by a small fire (v. 5) 

B. A world of unrighteousness (v. 6) 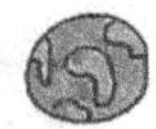

C. Set among our members (v. 6) 

D. Staining the whole body (v. 6) 

E. Sets on fire the whole course of life (v. 6) 

F. Set on fire by Hell (v. 6) 

G. Can not be tamed (v. 8)

H. A restless evil (v. 8) 

I. Full of deadly poison (v. 8) 

J. Used to bless our Lord and Father (v. 9) 

K. Used to curse people made in likeness of God (v. 9)

V. Paradoxes

    A. One mouth (v. 10) 

       a. Blessing (v. 10)

       b. Cursing (v. 10)

    B. A Spring (v. 11) 

       a. Fresh water (v. 11) 

       b. Salt water (v. 11) 

    C. Fig Tree (v. 12) 

       a. Bear olives (v. 12)  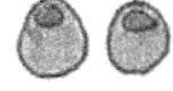

D. Grapevine (v. 12) 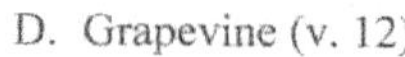

    a. Produce figs (v. 12) 

E. A Salt Pond (v. 12) 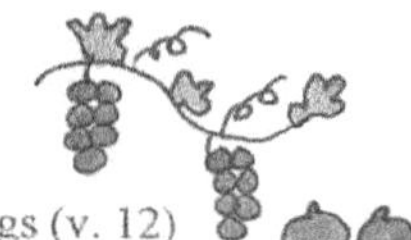

    a. Fresh water (v. 12) 

VI. The Wise and Understanding (v. 13) 

A. Good conduct (v. 13) 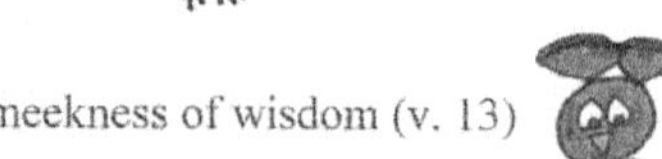

    a. Shows his works in the meekness of wisdom (v. 13) 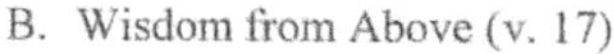

B. Wisdom from Above (v. 17)

    a. Pure (v. 17) 

    b. Peaceable (v. 17) 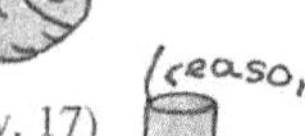

    c. Gentle (v. 17) 

    d. Open to reason (v. 17) 

    e. Full of mercy (v. 17) 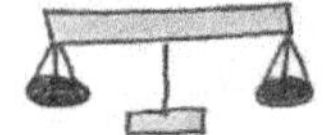

    f. Good fruits (v. 17) 

    g. Impartial (v. 17)

    h. Sincere (v. 17)

    i. A harvest of righteousness is sown in peace (v. 18) 

VII. Earthly Wisdom (v. 15) 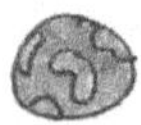

A. Stems from 

a.   Jealousy (v. 16)

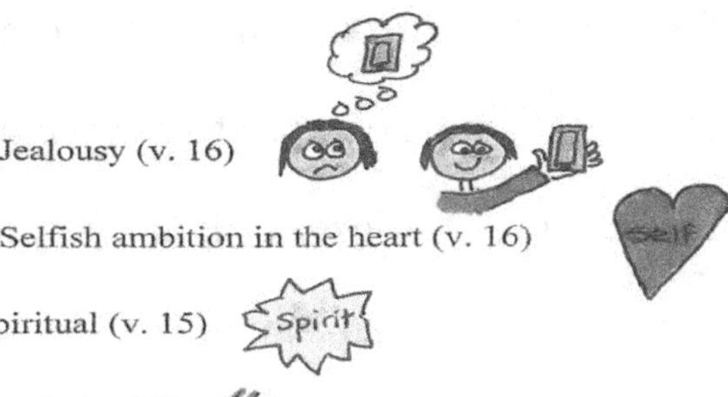

b.   Selfish ambition in the heart (v. 16)

B. Unspiritual (v. 15)

C. Demonic (v. 15)

D. Result

a.   Disorder (v. 16)

b.   Every vile practice (v. 16)

TRY IT YOURSELF!

This strategy works best when you use chunks of verses! Pick out a few verses, and see if you can use Roman numerals, letters, and numbers to jot down the main ideas from the verses. Then, add some pictures to help you remember the main ideas of the verses.

👁 **Style 4:** *Mind Maps:* A mind map is a helpful

tool for visual learners because they are non-linear,

meaning they do not utilize straight lines. Most of the

text that we typically read is in uniform, straight lines.

However, the brain is able to better process and

organize information when it is presented in a form

that is organic and free flowing, such as a mind map.

The way a mind map is created is through first placing

the central idea/topic in the center of the paper, and

then creating branches that flow out from the center

to break down the topic into small pieces. The mind

map that you see below is for James 4. The reference

is listed in the center as the central idea, and each of

the thick, colored branches have a key word that

represents the theme/key component of a chunk of

verses. The small, thin branches stemming out from

the thick branches break down the themes further

into one or two words to help you remember specific

words from the verses. The pictures are added as bonus hints! Use the key words and themes to help you piece together and memorize the chunks of verses in James 4.

Note: The following mind map is printed in black and white. If you would like free access to the color version of it so that you can print it out and use it, visit: https://sites.google.com/view/scriptureinstyleresources/home.

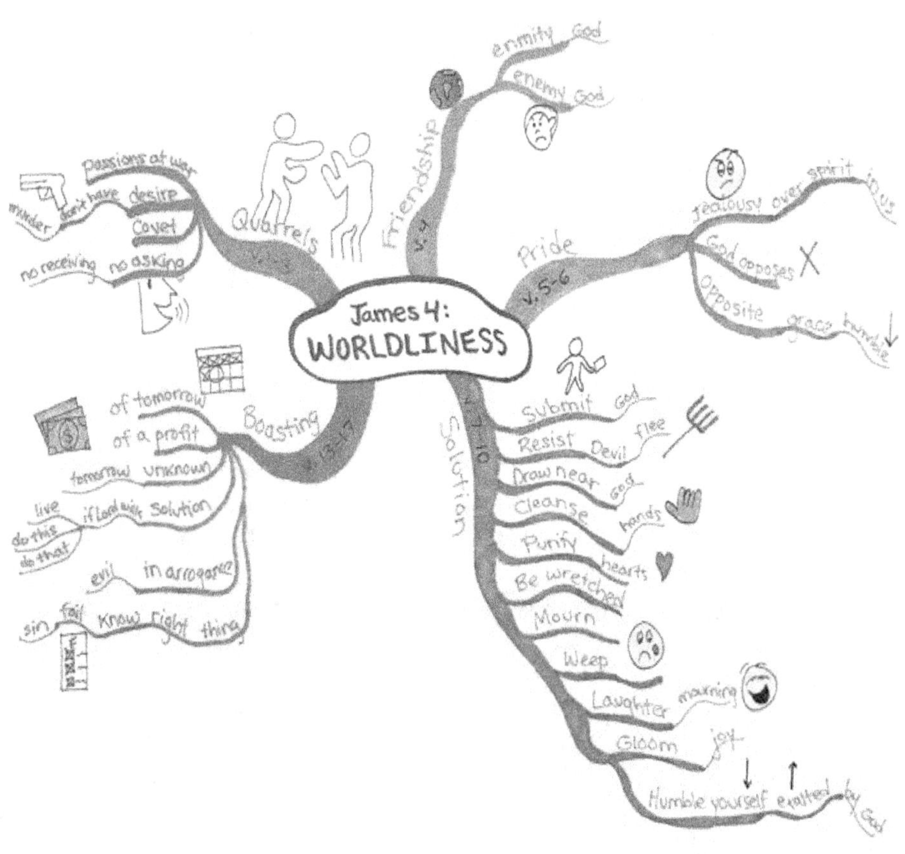

James 4: WORLDLINESS
Friendship v.4
enmity God
enemy God
Quarrels v.1-3
Passions at war
murder don't have desire
Covet
no receiving no asking
Pride v.5-6
jealousy over spirit in us
God opposes X
Opposite grace humble
Boasting v.13-17
of tomorrow
of a profit
tomorrow unknown
live if Lord wills Solution
do this
do that
evil in arrogance
sin fail know right thing
Solution v.7-10
Submit God
Resist Devil flee
Draw near God
Cleanse hands
Purify hearts
Be wretched
Mourn
Weep
Laughter mourning
Gloom joy
Humble yourself exalted by God

TRY IT YOURSELF!

Here is some space to create your own mind map! Make sure to place the verse's reference into the center circle, and then build colorful branches off of it to represent the key components/themes of the verse(s).

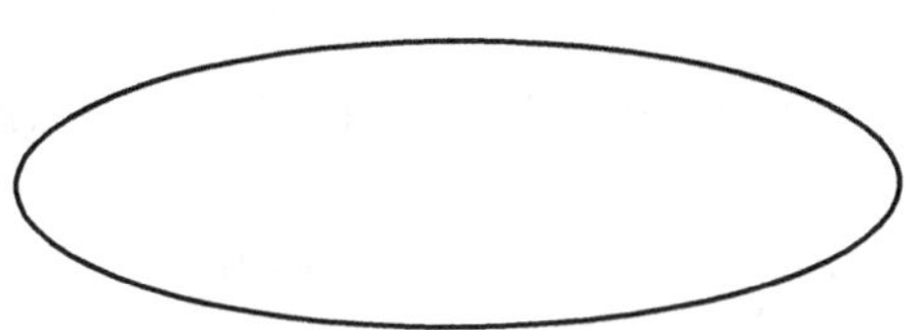

◉ **Style 5: *Sticky Notes:*** Let's be honest – sticky notes are probably one of the greatest inventions man has created that allows us to remember important things. Therefore, why not take this invention and use it for scripture memory! This style uses a set of sticky notes that contain words or pictures (or both!) that represent each verse, or group of verses in James 5. You take the sticky notes and place them around your house in a way that will allow you to walk around your house and recite the verses of the chapter in order as you see each sticky note. For example, you might hang some sticky notes around your bedroom, some in the hallway and some in the bathroom so that you see them when you walk from room to room. Your brain will benefit from having each word or picture associated with a location in your house. This memorizing style is perfect for a learner who is not only a visual learner, but a kinesthetic learner because it involves a visual component as well as a motion component. Again, you can start small by just using one or two sticky notes to memorize a few verses at a time to make it more manageable.

Note: The following sticky notes are printed in black and white. If you would like free access to the color version of them so that you can print them out and use them,
visit: https://sites.google.com/view/scriptureinstylere sources/home.

V. 1-3
Mine!
V. 4
Work harder!
LORD
We're not getting paid!
Help!
Help!
V. 5
Luxury self-indulgence
V. 6
rich
righteous
V. 7
V. 8
JESUS

V. 9
It's your fault!
No, you stole my idea!

V. 10-11
Steadfast
JOB
BLESSED

V. 12
They are stupid!
Yes!
No!

V. 13
Dear Jesus...

V. 13
La La La!

V. 14
Dear Jesus...
Dear Jesus...
Dear Jesus...

V. 15

V. 16

V. 17–18

V. 19–20

76

TRY IT YOURSELF!

Grab a pack of sticky notes. Write the reference to your verse on the back of one sticky note. Then on the front, draw an image, cut out an image from a magazine, or print out an image that represents your verse. Stick it in a place around your house where you will see it often! Do this several times on separate sticky notes for each verse or chunk of two or three verses that you want to memorize.

Quick Styles:

- Make your own fill in the blank cards by writing out a verse on an index card, leaving some words out. Go back later and see if you can fill in the missing words! Ex. John 3:16 (ESV) "For God so __________ the world, that he __________ his only ______, that whoever __________ in him should not perish but have

_________ _______.” You can create as many/little blanks as you want!

- Open up a new note on your phone and type a verse you recently learned.

To learn more about these and other memorizing ideas visit:

https://lifewaywomen.com/2019/06/18/how-to-memorize-scripture-memory-challenge/.

IN STYLE: AUDITORY LEARNERS

Auditory learners primarily learn new content through information that they can hear with their ears. They find sharing their thoughts, questions, and ideas with others, as well as receiving oral input in return particularly helpful when learning a new process or task. In addition, auditory learners do well when they can hear new information being told to them. For example, if an auditory learner is introduced to the life cycle of a frog, chances are he will learn the cycle most effectively through having another person explain each step verbally, in detail. Another example would be if an auditory learner is trying to figure out how much time he spends during the day on work, he will benefit from discussing the activities that he does in a day with another person, and then thinking through what percentage of his day work takes up. A lot of times auditory learners are verbal processors because they greatly benefit from hearing themselves talk situations out, while using the feedback from others to expand their perspective.

If you are an auditory learner, in school you probably learned best when you had assignments that required you to listen to new information or talk through new information with others. For example, maybe you learned best through listening to podcasts, listening to the audio version of your textbook, or through hearing your teacher give presentations or lectures. Perhaps as a child you greatly enjoyed asking the question, "Why?" to your parents and hearing them discuss principles of life. Or maybe you greatly enjoyed learning and listening to new songs, or you enjoyed hearing music playing in the background to help you focus on tasks.

Auditory learners are usually very "word" smart. In other words, auditory learners can be very skilled with using language because they have an understanding of how words can be used together, and they often engage in verbal conversation with others. For example, an auditory learner may be good at jobs involving debate, such as a lawyer, or jobs that involve music, such as a musician, a conductor, or a composer. Auditory learners may also do well with jobs that involve storytelling or translating. Having this knowledge, the rest of this chapter will be dedicated to providing examples of practical strategies for memorizing scripture that can be used by auditory learners.

Style 1: *Read to Me:* Download a Bible app in the version that you prefer and listen to the verses being read aloud to you, while looking at the text as it is being read. If you prefer, you can record yourself reading aloud the verses on your phone, and then replay the recording to listen to yourself reading the verses until you are able to remember them. Try adding verbal emphasis to a few important key words when you record yourself speaking the verses. For example, "Your *Word* is a *lamp* to my feet and a *light* to my path." (ESV) Then, listen to the recording all the time - when you are driving, when you are cooking dinner, and even when you are about to drift off to sleep.

Style 2: *Mindless Music:* In order to minimize distractions or eliminate background noise, auditory learners may find it helpful to turn on quiet piano music in the background while they are working on memorizing scripture. I have found it helpful to search, "soft piano background music", and usually several options are available to choose from. This music is very soothing and will allow learners to focus on reciting their memory verses aloud.

Style 3: ***Join a Memorization Group:*** Since auditory learners often learn best through engaging in conversations where they can talk through their thoughts and ideas with others, joining a scripture memorization group could prove to be a helpful strategy for auditory learners. Find a group near you who gathers in-person or online, for the purpose of reciting memorized scripture to each other. It can be as simple as meeting up once or twice a month and coming prepared to recite some verses that you have been memorizing. It is greatly encouraging to meet together and witness others who have devoted a great deal of time to memorizing the scriptures, just like you! I have discovered that there are many like-minded people in all parts of the U.S. that have a desire to memorize scripture, so there are many groups that already exist who meet on a regular basis. If you cannot find a group in your area, consider contacting one or two other like-minded people that you know and create your own scripture memorization group!

Style 4: *Try a Tune:* Learn verses through songs and tunes that others have already created. Upon doing some research, there are amazing songwriters out there who have invested their time into creating catchy songs to help people memorize scripture. Below are some of the musicians I came across and found helpful:

<u>*Seeds Family Worship*</u> - According to their website, they are a ministry that "creates scripture memory songs for kids by setting verses from the Bible to music."[11] Their mission is "to see God's Word, the Bible, planted in as many homes and hearts as possible around the world."[12] Even though their music is written primarily for kids, their tunes are very catchy and will assist adults in memorizing, as well! Their music can be accessed on all major music platforms. Check out their website for more

information:

https://www.seedsfamilyworship.com/.

Scripture Singer - This is an app that you can easily download on your phone, and it has over 250 Scripture songs that you can listen to. You can memorize scripture either by topic, or by searching up verses in a certain book of the Bible. To find out more information, check out their website:

https://www.scripturesinger.com.

Psallos - This is a group of musicians based in Jackson, TN. They are a group which "exists to create artistically excellent and theologically rich music (also like Psalms): melodies and lyrics that remind you of the truths of Scripture; harmonies, rhythms, and timbres that express the emotional weight of these truths."[13] So far, they have released Jude, Hebrews, and Romans to song. Annnnnd....the group is releasing their newest book of the Bible this year...Philippians!! Be sure to check out their website for more information at: https://www.psallos.com/.

Style 5: *Be a Music Maker:* If you are able to play an instrument and/or you like to sing, you can sing and play for the Lord in your own unique style, penning new songs and poems. This is a blessed thing, as Ephesians talks about, *"addressing one another in psalms and hymns and spiritual songs, singing and making melody to the Lord with your heart"* (Ephesians 5:19, ESV). It is a beautiful thing to make a joyful noise to the Lord (Ps 98:4) in whatever way He has gifted you. Start with a verse that has been particularly meaningful to you. Then, spend some quiet time with Jesus in prayer, and maybe even play around with some chords on your instrument. If you are listening, He will give you unique ways to worship Him!

TRY IT YOURSELF!

Select one of the auditory styles that you feel would be most beneficial to you. Fill in the following statement:

My goal is

____

_______________. I will achieve this goal

by____

_________________________________.

IN STYLE: KINESTHETIC LEARNERS

Kinesthetic learners primarily learn new content through working with their hands. They find the ability to hold and manipulate objects particularly helpful when learning a new process or task. For example, if a kinesthetic learner is introduced to the life cycle of a frog, chances are he will learn the cycle most effectively through taking part in the process by being given frog eggs to care for. The learner would take part in the experience by feeding and nurturing the eggs, watching each stage as they change into tadpoles, then young frogs, and finally adult frogs. Another example would be if a kinesthetic learner is trying to figure out if he is spending too many hours a day on work, he will benefit from using materials to build a representation that shows the amount of time spent on each activity in his day. This could look like using different quantities of objects, such as buttons and paper clips, to represent the number of hours spent on different activities during the day.

If you are a kinesthetic learner, in school you probably learned best when you had assignments that required you to build or create something, do experiments, or use practical knowledge. For example, maybe you learned best through role playing scenarios, watching your teacher model an activity, or taking field trips. Perhaps as a child you greatly enjoyed engaging in high energy activities, such as sports, dancing, or theater. Or maybe you greatly enjoyed tinkering around with machines and you desired to know how they worked, or you would build things out of materials you found in nature. Finally, maybe you really enjoyed playing house, or dressing up dolls and role-playing scenarios with them.

Kinesthetic learners are usually very "body" smart. In other words, kinesthetic learners can be very skilled with using movement because as they are active, their brains turn movements into pieces of knowledge. A kinesthetic learner may be good at jobs involving woodwork, medicine, plumbing, dancing, sports, or factory work, to name a few. Having this knowledge, the rest of this chapter will be dedicated to providing examples of practical strategies that kinesthetic learners can use for memorizing.

Style 1: *Model Memorizing:* Create something that helps you remember a set of verses. For example, maybe you are an artist who enjoys painting and you remember things best through making strokes on a canvas. This skill can be applied to scripture memory in that you can choose two or three verses that you are memorizing, and then you can create an image that reminds you of the verses. If you are a kinesthetic learner *and* a visual learner, you may find this even more useful, as it brings in a visual aspect, as well. Another example would be applying scripture memory to woodworking, or photography. If you enjoy woodworking, you could sculpt a representation out of wood to remind you of the verses. If you enjoy photography, you could shoot a series of photographs that remind you of the verses you are memorizing. As you are working on building or creating the image, you can quote the scripture in

your mind, thus solidifying it further.

Style 2: *Location is Everything:* Study your scripture memory verses in a unique location that allows you to manipulate your body. A majority of the time, when I did schoolwork, I found myself sitting on a chair or on my couch. While this can be effective for some, kinesthetic learners may find it more stimulating to learn new verses by thinking of different ways to position themselves. For example, maybe you are a dancer and you enjoy coming up with your own motions that are representative of ideas. Or maybe you enjoy working out, so you memorize best when you are able to engage your body by doing push-ups or going for a jog while reciting your verses. There are tons of different ways that you can engage your body in the memorization process through motion. You just have to choose which one works best for your liking.

Style 3: *Move Those Limbs:* Study your scripture memory verses by engaging your body through tapping your hands, feet, or legs in some way. It may sound odd, but personally, I read and comprehend new things best when I am able to tap my pencil against my paper as I am reading. While it may be annoying to the people around you, it can be a simple way of adding some motion to rote reading or speaking.

Style 4: *Act It Out:* Learn the scriptures through theater! Maybe you are an actor or actress, and you enjoy writing skits. You could grab a friend or two and create a skit that applies the message that the set of verses is trying to convey, and then you could both recite the verses at the end of the skit to reinforce the concepts. For example, maybe you are memorizing the passage in James 2 that talks about showing no partiality to those who are rich. You could easily reenact verses 2-7, having one person be a rich man, one person being a poor man, and one person being a bystander telling them where to sit or stand. After the drama, you could create a statement saying how it applies to your life, and then finally recite the verses.

 **Style 5: *Do the Hop!*** Learn the scriptures

through hopscotch! Go out on

your driveway or the sidewalk

in front of your house and use

sidewalk chalk to draw a

typical hopscotch board. This

is no longer just a game for

children! Try hopping one

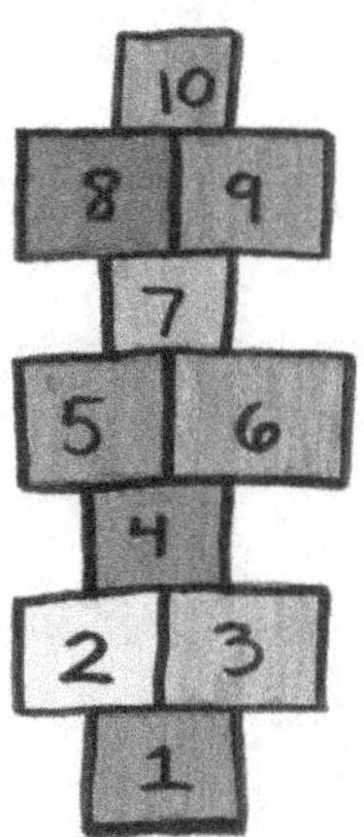

square at a time for each word you say. For example,

for James 1:1 you would hop on square one and say,

"James", then you would hop on square two and say,

"1" and then the next square you would say "1", so on

and so forth: *"James"* (hop), "a" (hop), "servant"

(hop), etc.

TRY IT YOURSELF!

Now, select one of the kinesthetic styles that you feel would be most beneficial to you. Fill in the following statement: My goal is

____

__________________. I will achieve this goal by

____

___________________________.

MEMORIZING AS A WAY OF LIFE

As I look back on my life, I exude extreme gratitude towards my parents for the seed of God's Word they sewed into me from a young age, even before I made a personal decision to memorize much of God's Word. The church that I attended while growing up had a Bible Memory Program that children could participate in from kindergarten through eighth grade. Each year, from January through May, participants were sent home with a large, yellow packet of verses that lasted fifteen weeks. They memorized three to five verses per week, and the verse length and complexity varied as your grade level went up. In 7th and 8th grade, participants received a list of verse references, and they had to look up the verses, write them down, and then memorize them. Every fifth week of the program was a review week.

This is no small feat. My sister and I were one of a few children who went through the whole program K-8th grade. I largely contribute this success to the dedication of my parents, and especially my Dad, as he purposely incorporated scripture memory into my daily life. I remember days where I would swing on my swing set in the backyard, and my Dad would push me, and he would have me say my verses. Other times, we would sit in the living room and he would have my sister and I sit in the "hot seat," which was a fancy way of saying that you sat in the recliner while he asked you your verses. When a tough verse would come up, my Dad would put it to music so that it was easier to remember. He had a gift for this! One of the verses was Ephesians 4:32, and he put that one to the tune of "Row, Row, Row Your Boat". Putting the words to song had a lasting effect; to this day, I still never forget Ephesians 4:32. To spice it up a little bit, he would suggest that we (him, my sister, and I) sing the verse in a round, like you would sing "Row, Row, Row Your Boat" in music class. Unlike most kids in the Bible memory program who only had a few review weeks, every week was a review week for us. My dad not only asked us to say the new verses we had learned that week, but also the ones from the previous weeks. I know that not every child had parents who put as much time and energy into the program as my Dad did, and for that I thank the Lord.

The verses from the Bible Memory Program have stuck with me years later, and have become like old, faithful friends on challenging days. I encourage you in this - memorizing scripture does not have to be a complicated experience. Deuteronomy 6:7 says, *"Repeat them [the commandments and the Law of God] again and again to your children. Talk about them when you are at home and when you are on the road, when you are going to bed and when you are getting up"* (NLT). God's Word and the laws of God are meant to be dwelt upon amidst our everyday activities. In this passage, Moses is reminding the Israelites to repeatedly speak to their children about the laws of God so that they are in the forefront of their minds. Moses then gives practical examples of how this can be done, with the first being to talk about them when you are at home. My parents set a great example for me when I was growing up. When I struggled with a situation at school, my parents would remind me what God's Word says and then help me apply it to my situation in a very practical manner. For example, I would often have conflicts with my best friend who would abandon me to hang out with another one of our mutual friends instead. I would explain to my parents what was happening, and then they would remind me that Jesus is a friend who sticks closer than a brother (Proverbs 18:24), and that if I felt lonely, I could always talk to Jesus about it because He was always with me. Applying scripture verses to real-life situations is one of the best ways to *"be transformed by the renewal of your mind"* (Romans 12:2 ESV).

The second way Moses instructs the Israelites is to talk about God's Word when they are on the road. Back then they did not have cars where they could drive from place to place, so they probably had lots of time to talk as they walked from place to place. In today's world we instead go from place to place frequently in our cars, whether that's to work, the grocery store, picking up the kids, or to the gym. We can view this travel time as an essential part of our day to process the events of our day in light of the scriptures.

There are four simple ways to put this into action:

1. Simply write down a verse that God has been speaking to you about and tape it on the dashboard of your car. Read it when you get in the car.

2. Ask your kids, *"How was your day?"* When you hear what they say, good or bad, you can encourage them with a verse that pertains to their situation, reminding them that Jesus is with them.

3. Listen to a Christian radio station that plays worship music with lyrics that were penned based on the truths found in the Bible.

4. Listen to a Christian podcast or sermon on our phone as you drive along. Choose a pastor that you really enjoy and pop that on the radio.

I am thankful that Moses added this portion about remembering God's Word during our travel time because it tells me that the time that we spend traveling has value and can be used to grow our relationship with God.

Finally, Moses instructs the Israelites to talk about God's Word when they are going to bed and when they are getting up. It has the idea that dwelling on God's Word is a continual process -- it does not end when we go to bed or when we are moving from place to place. It continues on throughout our whole life. We can do this by spending time in our Bibles in the morning when we first wake up, and in the evening before we go to sleep. How will we be able to repeat the laws and precepts of God and talk about them when we do not have them in our minds and hearts? This is the danger, friends. We cannot use what we do not already have access to. You cannot withdraw money that you do not have. This is why it is so important that we are not forsaking daily time spent with God, reading His Word, and continually asking ourselves how it applies to us. After a year of intentionally doing this, it will become part of your way of life. As the old saying goes, *"A Bible that's falling apart usually belongs to a person who is not."* How true!

ACCOUNTABILITY

In order to embed scripture memory into your daily life, one of the greatest assets you can have is accountability along the way. One of my fondest experiences memorizing scripture was in partnership with my dear friend, Stephanie. At the time, we were separated by distance, as she was attending college in Ohio, and I was attending college in Pennsylvania. Before she left for college, we determined that we were going to do a weekly phone call on Wednesday evenings to keep in touch throughout the semester. As Stephanie and I were having our weekly catch-up one evening, she mentioned how she was engaged in a study on Ephesians with a small group of girls, and she had decided to go ahead and memorize the book. When I heard that, I jumped on the bandwagon and told her that I wanted to memorize it along with her!

We decided to each take time during our week to memorize a few verses individually, and then each Wednesday night when we did our catch-up, we would indeed catch up, and then we would recite Ephesians together. One of us would start out, and then after a few verses, the other person would pick it up. If one of us got stuck at a certain point, the other could provide a clue, or jump in and pick it up. Why do I take time to share this anecdote? I have pulled four takeaways from this season with my dear friend that I believe will encourage you in your scripture memory journey. 1) Memorize God's Word with a friend or relative that shares your same desire to memorize. Ecclesiastes 4:9-10 (NLT) says *"Two people are better than one, for they can help each other succeed. If either of them falls down, one can help the other up. But pity anyone who falls and has no one to help them up."* When memorizing scripture alone, especially if your aim is to memorize large portions, it is easy to lose motivation or steam after a while. I have seen this in my own life, especially when memorizing full books of scripture that have several chapters. The beautiful thing about memorizing it with a friend or relative is that when one of you starts to lose motivation, the other person can provide encouragement and maybe even a friendly text or call as a reminder to get back into it. 2) Set up a specific time each week that works for both of you that will be dedicated to reciting the passage you have learned. I have found it is important to prioritize scripture memory, just like I would any other commitment I have, otherwise it does not get done in the busyness of life. One solution that has been helpful for me is to mark the time on my calendar or to set a reminder on my phone. Technology makes this so easy for us nowadays. 3) Pray for each other as you memorize

God's Word together. It is always encouraging when you know that someone is praying for you in any aspect of life. You can pray for your partner, that the *"God of our Lord Jesus Christ, the Father of glory, may give them the Spirit of wisdom and of revelation in the knowledge of him"* (Eph. 1:17 ESV) as they study the Word. 4) Share testimonies with each other about what God is teaching you as you meditate upon His Word through memorization. Revelation 12:11 (ESV) says, *"They [the saints in Christ] have conquered him [Satan] by the blood of the Lamb and by the word of their testimony."* When we speak of the things the Lord has done for us, it encourages us because we *remember* what He has done for us, causing us to turn toward Him with grateful hearts. In addition, remembering how He has been faithful to us in the past serves as one of our greatest means of triumphing over the enemy's desire to throw attacks

at us.

ENCOURAGEMENT

Now that you are equipped with the strategies you need for memorizing scripture according to your learning style, I want to share one of the benefits of the hard work, time, and effort you put in. The Lord uses those who memorize scripture to encourage the people around them. I have witnessed it firsthand numerous times. I'll never forget, in 2018 my Community College's Christian Fellowship Club was on the way down to Corpus Christi, Texas to provide relief to the victims of Hurricane Harvey. I was sitting on a plane next to my friend Ryan, who, unbeknownst to me would later become my husband, and we were passing the time asking each other Bible trivia questions. At the time, I had recently begun memorizing Paul's letter to the Ephesians. Realizing that once we got to Texas I would not have much time to practice, I asked Ryan if I could recite to him what I had learned so far so he could correct any mistakes. He agreed, so I recited Ephesians 1 and part of Ephesians 2. His response was surprising to me. He was blown away because he had never met anyone who memorized large chunks of scripture like this! Now I do not share this story to gloat and make myself look talented. I share it for a couple reasons. One, because Ryan told me later that this was greatly encouraging to him, and that it challenged him in his faith to begin to meditate and dwell on the Word continually. Two, I share the story because it went further than just me reciting scripture to Ryan. When you are on a plane, you are in close proximity to the people around you. That means oftentimes you can overhear what the person in the next seat is saying. When I was finished reciting Ephesians, I will never forget, but I looked up, and the man sitting in the row in front of us had a Bible resting on his lap. When we landed, he turned around and said to me, "What a blessing to hear you guys reciting scripture!" It turns out he and his family were missionaries, but wow! What an incredible opportunity for God to speak through you when you speak His living Word into the atmosphere around you. It brings encouragement, hope, and life to the people it reaches. And maybe, just maybe, you will garner a spouse along the way.

UPLIFT

I wrote previously about how God uses those who memorize scripture to encourage the people around them, and I referenced how I have seen Him use it to encourage those already in the body of Christ. However, it is also important to mention that God uses those who memorize scripture to uplift the non-Christians around them, if they are willing to speak up. Being a more introverted person, I have often struggled to be courageous with evangelizing and stopping to pray for the people around me when I feel led by the Holy Spirit. However, when I do step out in faith in these areas, I have seen that God so faithfully brings to mind the scriptures I have memorized and meditated on in the past, even if I memorized them several months or years ago.

I know I will always think of the book of James fondly as my firstborn, and yes, I do mean like a child, because it was the first book of scripture the Lord called me to memorize. If you have children, you know there is just something unique about that first experience birthing a child! But I digress. I was memorizing James chapter two, where he is talking about how as followers of Christ we need to be doers of the Word, and not hearers only (v. 22). There is a warning here for us to heed! If we are just hearers of the Word, then we are like a man who looks at his face in a mirror and then goes away and forgets what he looks like. To put it another way, it is like when someone tells you something important and it goes in one ear and out the other. The information is not changing the way you live; it is not transforming your life. Around the same time I was memorizing this section, one of my professors came into class crying because she was upset about a situation that was going on in her life. At that moment, my heart went out to her and I felt a prompting to share Jesus with her, but I was scared! As I continued to work on memorizing this section in James and meditating on what it meant for my life, the Holy Spirit brought to mind Romans 10:14, *"How then will they call on him in whom they have not believed? And how are they to believe in him of whom they have never heard? And how are they to hear without someone preaching?"* (ESV) with the gentle prompting that means, *"You need to go!"*

One day I finally went into my professor's office, literally legs shaking as I walked up the steps to get there. My voice was shaking too, but I just simply let her know that when she was upset it touched me and I began to speak about Jesus. As I was speaking, the Holy Spirit was bringing verses to my mind to share with her. I talked to her about how I was once lost in sin, but now I am a new creation; the old is passed, and the new has come (2 Corinthians 5:17). I also felt led to ask her if she had ever heard John 3:16 before. (If you do not know it, please look it up! It is a beautiful verse that is often taken for granted because of its familiarity in the church.) She had never heard it before, so I proceeded to quote it to her from memory. There are lots of points that could be made from this story, but the point I want to make here is this: When you take the time to sit with Jesus and put His Word into your mind and your heart, since you have the mind of Christ, the Holy Spirit can bring it to your mind at any time when you need it. I did not know which verses would uplift my professor at that moment, but the Holy Spirit who searches hearts did, and was able to bring those exact ones to my mind, why? I had deliberately taken time to put them in my mind at a previous time. It is a wonderful benefit when you are evangelizing and praying for the lost and you do not have your Bible with you! Furthermore, I could speak 1,000 of my own words and they all would fall to the ground because they are not eternal, but I know that the Word of God does not return void (Isaiah 55:11). This means that God's Word always accomplishes its divine purposes, even if we cannot see the result at that exact moment when we pray for someone or share the Gospel with someone. God's Word is a powerful means of uplifting the soul and spirit of those who have never had a personal encounter with Jesus Christ.

CONCLUSION

As you can probably tell, memorizing scripture is not for the faint of heart! It takes time, dedication, hard work, and much practice. Even so, once you have identified your learning style, memorizing scripture in accordance with this preferred style will make all the difference in your journey of memorizing. I know the Bible can look big and intimidating at times because of its sheer size, but I promise, if you take one verse at a time, you will be on your way. Text or call one of your Christian friends who will work on memorizing with you and will help hold you accountable. Start with a verse that impacted you during your quiet time and try memorizing it today!

The enemy, Satan, is always prowling around, looking for someone to devour (1 Peter 5:8). If you are not vigilant in protecting your heart and mind with the sword of the Spirit, which is God's Word, then it is easy for him to get a foothold in your life. When you know the scriptures, you are then able to recognize the lies Satan speaks to your heart and mind, and you are then able to take a stand with God's Word and let Satan know the truth! Once you have resisted the devil, he will flee from you (James 4:7).

Step out bravely onto the battleground with God's Word hidden in your heart and the sword of the Spirit in hand. You will find that you are able to greatly encourage and uplift the people around you. Fear not, for you have been given the mind of Christ in all circumstances! Let's become like David, who, though he stumbled at times, dearly held onto God's Word in all seasons of life, thus being named a man after God's own heart. Won't you begin today?

NOTES

[1] David Guzik, "Study Guide for 1 Samuel 26 by David Guzik," Blue Letter Bible, accessed January 2021, https://www.blueletterbible.org/Comm/archives/guzik_david/StudyGuide_1Sa /1Sa_26.cfm.

[2] Arthur T. Pierson, *George Müller of Bristol* (Grand Rapids, Michigan: The Zondervan Corporation, 1984), 106.

[3] "Strong's Hebrew Lexicon (ESV)," Blue Letter Bible, accessed January 2021, https://www.blueletterbible.org//lang/lexicon/lexicon.cfm?Strongs=H6845&t=ESV.

[4] Leland Ryken, James C. Wilhoit, Tremper Longman III, *Dictionary of Biblical Imagery* (Downers Grove, Illinois: InterVarsity Press, 1998), 817.

[5] Marc La Porte, "Consider This!," Deurpost, February 10, 2010, accessed January 2021, https://deurpost.wordpress.com/2010/02/11/consider-this/.

[6] "The World Watch List: The Top 50 Countries Where Its Most Difficult to Follow Jesus," Open Doors, accessed January 2021, https://www.opendoorsusa.org/christian-persecution/world-watch-list/.

[7] Grace, "Strengthen What Remains...," Open Doors, June 5, 2013, accessed February 2021, https://www.opendoorsusa.org/christian-persecution/stories/strengthen-what-remains/.

8 David Guzik, "Study Guide for Revelation 3 by David Guzik," Blue Letter Bible, accessed January 2021, https://www.blueletterbible.org/Comm/guzik_david/StudyGuide2017-Rev/Rev-3.cfm.

9 Matt Slick, "Which Bible version is the best?," Christian Apologetics & Research Ministry, May 15, 2010, accessed January 2021, https://carm.org/which-bible-version-is-best.

10 David Mathis, "Five Tips for Bible Memory," Desiring God, February 9, 2015, accessed January 2021, https://www.desiringgod.org/articles/five-tips-for-bible-memory.

11 "Seeds Family Worship Mission," Seedsfamilyworship.com, accessed January 2021.

12 Ibid.

13 "About Psallos," Psallos.com, accessed January 2021.

PERMISSIONS

Sharing Content for Profit-Related Activities: Blue Letter Bible

Users have permission to cite and provide excerpts found on BLB for use in profit-related activities, such as the publication of books, media, and other resources. Users must request permission to use significant portions of resources (over 500 words). Such permission must be granted by BLB or outside teachers, authors, and ministries, as is stated in the sections below.

Guidelines for BLB Sharing Content

The following guidelines represent the requirements needed to share content from BLB. To see whether permission is needed to share specific types of content see the Content Sharing Guidelines section.

1. Users may not alter the content in any way.
2. Users may not charge any fees or other remuneration when sharing or redistributing content. If a fee is charged, special permission must be granted.
3. Users must give appropriate attribution such as what is offered by the citation feature.
4. If it is a website, users must hyperlink "Blue Letter Bible" to https://www.blueletterbible.org/.
5. If it is a website, users must hyperlink the content page link to the specific URL where the content lives.

Dictionary of Biblical Imagery

Copyright Protection

All materials published by InterVarsity Press are protected by copyright. Therefore, in instances not excepted by the "fair use" clause (see below), you will need written permission before you can reproduce IVP materials in any form including, but not limited to, the following:

- photocopying or retyping
- reprinting in a book, magazine, or other publication
- recording and/or storing in audio or electronic formats
- translating
- creating derivative materials, such as study guides, book summaries, or videos (to name a few)

Fair Use

The "fair use" clause of current US copyright law allows you to reproduce short excerpts from copyrighted works (our standard is less than 500 words) with standard footnoting. The "fair use" clause also allows you to make one copy of selected material from a copyrighted work for personal use only (e.g., for your own study or reference). "Fair use" applies to the content of InterVarsity publications and the IVP Online website. Hymns, poems, and illustrations such as cartoons, maps, tables, or charts are usually considered complete pieces, which means that you will need written permission even though they may contain less than 500 words.

Permission for CARM
Hello Hannah,

Thanks for your email. Thanks for writing to CARM.
My name is Tim and I am a volunteer who helps to
answer emails for this website.

You are welcome to cite Matt Slick's articles, as long
as you follow the guidelines listed
here. https://carm.org/carm/copying-linking-and-
citing-carm/

Tim
CARM

1. **You may copy** articles and place them in your
   church bulletins, newsletters, etc. in non-
   electronic format.
2. **Quotations of CARM articles in books
   and magazines** are allowed (and encouraged)
   provided the proper documentation is given.
   1. One article may be reproduced for each
      book and magazine. Beyond this
      permission is required from CARM.
3. **You may copy** parts of carm articles for use
   in emails as long as the emails do not end up
   on websites. Again, we do not want search
   engines to find CARM articles anywhere except
   CARM.
4. **Fair use laws** state that small portions of
   material may be quoted for documentation
   purposes, without written permission, but
   must be unaltered and accompanied by the
   proper documentation citing the source.

Permission for Lifeway women source:

---------- Forwarded message ---------

From: **Connie Swinehart**
<connie.swinehart@lifeway.com>
Date: Fri, Feb 12, 2021 at 11:41 AM
Subject: Re: Misc. Permission Request Submitted 2/10/2021 19:06:21

If you are only using the text and word count described in your email, permission can be granted for this to be done for your book, not for any other distribution. Please use the copyright as it is listed in the article and add "Reprinted and used by permission."

Connie Swinehart
Legal Coordinator
Lifeway Christian Resources

Permission from Marc La Porte:

Marc La Porte commented on Consider This!.

in response to **Hannah A**:

Great article! Is there a way I can request permission to use a quote from this article in my own published book? Please let me know! Thank you!

No problem, Hannah!

Permission for the George Müller book:
---------- Forwarded message ---------
From: **HCCPpermissions** <HCCPpermissions@har
percollins.com>
Date: Thu, Feb 4, 2021 at 2:33 PM
Subject: RE: Permissions Form - Hannah Armbruster

Dear Hannah,

Thank you for your recent request for permission to
reproduce material from the publication *"George
Müller of Bristol"*.

 Our records indicate that this title is now in the
public domain and you may quote/reprint from it
without permission. Please keep in mind that using an
author's exact words without attribution can
constitute plagiarism, even if the material is in the
public domain. Therefore, it is always necessary to
cite the source of the material. Also, please note that
the public domain nature does not apply to any
images or formatting of the book

 Thank you,

 Alison

 Alison McEmber
Subsidiary Rights Manager

Licensing & Subsidiary Rights

P.O. Box 141000
Nashville, Tennessee 37214

Permission from Open Doors:
---------- Forwarded message ---------
From: **Ryan Hamm** <ryanh@odusa.org>
Date: Thu, Feb 18, 2021 at 4:48 PM
Subject: Re: Permission Request

Dear Ms. Armbruster:

 We're happy to grant permission to use our research—in fact, if you're just citing our research, there's no need to get permission for this type of usage.

Sincerely,

Ryan Hamm

Editorial Director

Open Doors USA

Permission from David Mathis:

---------- Forwarded message ---------
From: **David Mathis** <david.mathis@desiringgod.org>
Date: Tue, Feb 16, 2021 at 6:07 PM
Subject: Re: Permission Request
To: Hannah Armbruster

Thank you, Hannah. I'm honored, and how very kind of you to check. What a fantastic topic for a book, and I pray for God's richest blessings on it!

David

Permission from Seeds Family Worship:
---------- Forwarded message ---------
From: **Josh
Houser** <josh@seedsfamilyworship.com>
Date: Sat, Feb 6, 2021 at 10:42 AM
Subject: Re: Permission Request
To: Hannah Armbruster
Cc: Seeds Family Worship
<seeds@seedsfamilyworship.com>

Absolutely! Totally approved! Thanks for sharing about Seeds. We are so grateful.
Blessings!
josh

Joshua Houser
Seeds Family Worship Missionary
406-250-0004
josh@seedsfamilyworship.com

Permission from Cody Curtis:

---------- Forwarded message ---------
From: **Psallos Music** <psallosmusic@gmail.com>
Date: Thu, Feb 11, 2021 at 10:57 AM
Subject: Re: Permission Request
To: Hannah Armbruster

Hannah,

Attached is the license granting you permission. Let me know if you need anything else.

Blessings to you with your book!

Grace and peace,
Cody

I, Cody Curtis, the Director of and copyright owner of Psallos, grant Hannah Armbruster permission to include our website, www.psallos.com, in her book, entitled "Scripture in Style: A Guide to Memorizing Scripture According to Your Learning Style."

Signature _______________________________   Date 2/11/2021

Permission from Scripture Singer:

Scripture Singer
Craig Cleveland
6040 Reese Hill Road
Sumas, WA 98295

March 19, 2021

Hannah Armbruster

Dear Hannah,
We would be happy for you to reference our app and
ministry in your book as requested.
Thank you, indeed, for choosing this wonderful
topic—God's Word!
May God bless your book and its distribution!

Sincerely,
Craig Cleveland
President, Scripture Singer
www.ScriptureSinger.com

ABOUT THE AUTHOR

 HANNAH ARMBRUSTER is a recent graduate from DeSales University with her bachelor's degree in Elementary Education. She has experience working as an academic coach, tutor, and Bible study leader. Currently, she teaches at an elementary school and lives in Philadelphia with her husband, Ryan. In her free time, she enjoys reading, crafting, studying scripture, and baking. She is passionate about equipping young women with tools for studying scripture and helping them grow in their walk with Jesus Christ.